CHAOS TO CONTROL!

...so business can be plain sailing

**All Systems Go For
Productivity, Proficiency & Profitability.**

7 steps to plugging your "leaky buckets" by eliminating inefficiency and waste, and therefore making more money in the process!

Clive I. Jones
Turbocharging Business Systematically

Chaos To Control!
(All Systems Go for Plain Sailing)

Copyright © 2017 by Clive I. Jones

No Part of this book may be used or reproduced in any manner whatsoever without prior permission from the author.

Disclaimer

For clarity and conciseness here are the two most important legalities regarding this book in plain English.
1. The reader assumes all responsibility of this publication for the use of these materials and information.
2. This book is not intended as legal or financial advice.

ISBN :
ISBN-13: 978-1974649174
ISBN-10: 1974649172
First Edition
All Systems Go Revised

Published by:
Clive Jones

www.jonesci.com.au

Dedicated to all who have helped me to gain the experience I have shared here.

Contents

Introduction

1. Why Do Organisations Waste So Much Time Energy and Money?
2. The 7 step process
3. Judgement.
4. Organisation.
5. Numbers.
6. Efficacy.
7. Systemology.
8. Collaboration.
9. Innovation.
10. Making It All Work.
11. Your Jonesci Charter.
12. Credit Where It's Due.

Introduction

Is Your Business Flowing Freely?

Or is it held back by inefficiencies, and wasted energy?

Let me set the picture for you. Come with me on an exciting journey.

Being a keen sailor I will take you on board a nice yacht. You can forget the daily grind, relax, and put some focus into your important part of the world. It's amazing how easy it can be when outside your normal routine.

On this journey there will be some comparisons made, between life on board the yacht, and those of your life in the business world. In fact, on my Nautical PowWows program, I do actually take you on a yacht Charter and help you develop your own agreement (or Charter). Corny play on words...yes I know but bear with me...you'll get used to it, and there's more to come.

My intention is to get you to question the status quo.... that which you probably accept as either normal, or something too far beyond your control to be able make any difference. I'm here to tell you that you can! At least I have, and I don't believe I have anything extra in my advantage so what I share here, you can use yourself.

Every business I have worked in since being a young apprentice, (and yes there have been many over the 30 plus years) has had considerable amounts of wastage... haemorrhaging time and money everywhere.

Time was wasted through repeat work, blockages and bottlenecks, unnecessary meetings, lack of direction, procrastination...the list goes on.

Then there is the hard cost of wasted materials, excess stocks, unsold product, money left on the table...and again the list goes on.

The hidden costs of recruitment – or re-recruitment when someone leaves, re-training, low moral, distractions and more again.

Are you thinking "Ouch!" to each of these points?

Most businesses have money flowing in, but flowing out just as rapidly through all these leaks, but typically the main aim is to keep tipping more in the top…. which of course needs to happen so the bank doesn't dry up.

The flow is choked causing pressures at other areas in the business finding weak points in which energy is expended unnecessarily.

Imagine if you were on this nice yacht and it had barnacles on the bottom, the sails were worn, or the engine was a bit unreliable. What if some of the crew didn't perform their roles correctly at the right time because they didn't know how to, or had their own ideas. Maybe you set off but weren't prepared for what the weather was going to throw at you, or even what direction to steer to get where you want to go. Compare this to a well maintained yacht, with an efficient crew following a tried and tested system, all understanding their roles and responsibilities, and working to a well thought out plan. It would be whole lot more effective wouldn't it? And more fun too!

So in your business life, what would be the outcome if we started fixing those weak points, and then were continuing to fill up the "bucket"... of course it would start to fill up and eventually overflow – maybe into another bucket, or two, or three!

So why do we all have these leaky buckets? In most cases I have found that the leaks have not been the focus...maybe an irritation, but the sums have not been done to realise how much is leaking each day, and then how much that adds up to. Perhaps sometimes the realisation is there, except there is no-one to plug them, or the knowledge of how to fix them is missing.

I have read many books and learned from a lot of people... a whole atlas full of roadmaps to achieve a wide range of different things that we all need to learn in business, and realise that to many, it is simply a case of so much to do and so little time.... so where do I start?

Being a bit of a logical kind of guy, I have always set out to find the easy and most reliable way for things to happen. This book is my attempt to help you through this challenge in a logical process... a system or framework to follow if you like.

For most, they have poor or no systems in place to make the business run efficiently in the first place so are often at the ransom of expensive employees helping them to hold things together. With systems in place we have less reliance on employee intelligence and can have more accountability to ensure tasks are completed properly.

I've been a mad keen yacht racer and a Yacht-Master Instructor for about 30 years, and I can't help running the comparison of how in that pastime we have countless systems and processes to follow, and to be able to reach the top in the sport these are simply refined more and more as the competition grows.

From simple checklists to make sure we have all the safety gear on board, and briefing all crew-members where it's stowed... through to the obvious... plotting the race or voyage so we know where we are headed. Imagine that.. just wandering down the dock, casting off and setting sail... without having any kind of a plan or system to follow.

Even for that initial activity there is a need for a process or system to follow... we need to check a few things before starting the motor, then, when it's on do we have cooling water running through it...check...

OK, so is everyone in position, which way is the wind and current going to push the boat when we cast off, so which ropes are not needed and can be let go first, and which ones do we use to make sure we keep the boat under control.

We haven't left the dock yet and the process goes on... yet an average team following a simple system can make it look blissfully easy. I've been on board with both and I can tell you which I'd prefer. When you know how to do it correctly...it's mildly entertaining to watch a bunch of heroes stuffing it up as they charge off without any organisation. Being a Sailing Instructor too – it's also a little irritating at the same time.

I come from a family of business owners, manufacturers, engineers, and service professionals and my background from leaving school has been in business management.... theory and practical experience combined.

I've run my own businesses since 1993 and prior to that had a knack of making my jobs run independently of me.

Let's think about that for a moment... how would it be for you to make yourself redundant in the daily functions of working IN your own business or department.... so that you can actually spend time developing the future and helping your team fine tune it further every week.

That's not to say of course as the CEO, Director, Manager or Proprietor, that you can't go and play in it and do the routine things you like to do... but you do then have the choices.

You might be a department manager like I was, and want to enjoy your work, and have the opportunity to work more strategically, running the best operation rather than constantly fighting fires and going home stressed every day. Leader's roles are to ensure their teams follow appropriate systems, and to step up when the system is inadequate, such as when exceptions to the rule crop up.

I once had a job managing Inventory and Freight, which was in a mess when I started. After a short while the MD realised I had that all under control so he gave my bosses job to me, running Purchasing and Production as well...promotion!! I therefore had to set about systemising those roles too and before long I was knocking off again at 4pm (to go yacht racing of course) with everything done and all going smoothly.... no stress, no unpaid work, and a great social life because I could get out of work on time and relax knowing everything was under control.

Do you have a goal or two? Are you working towards achieving those goals? It's surprising how effective you become when you have the drive to achieve something you want.

Enjoying a challenge I jumped straight into another job where  they had a major stock control issue. $12M worth of computer hardware and software... all the popular stuff.... and only 48% accuracy in the computer... a disaster waiting to happen. A simple systematic approach to identifying errors, mainly procedural, and putting systems or procedures in place, from Sales, through to Accounts, Purchasing, Goods in, Despatch, Returns, Management... the list goes on, we lifted the accuracy to 99.8% at the following stock-take. I tend to get bored when successful and things have started working for me, so decided I needed a bigger challenge and started working for myself.

As a Business and Executive Coach and Consultant for the last 20 plus years, I have spent most of my time helping Business leaders and owners just like you to develop and implement systems into their businesses, with the aim of eliminating inefficiencies and therefore giving them the freedom to choose whether they work or not.

"Insanity is doing the same thing over and over again, expecting different results".

One of my favourite things is "Leverage", and I'm constantly thinking, how can we use the power of leverage to benefit this business or situation.

Just like putting a crowbar under an object to give you more power to move it, or a set of pulley blocks to decrease the amount of energy or effort you need to apply when pulling the rope when sailing, I like to explore and create systems and processes whereby once established, your work is done, and you can get your team to do it... consistently over and over again.

Using this leverage to ensure waste and inefficiencies are minimised or eliminated is what the Jonesci Charter is all about.

My goal in producing this book is to share with you my methodologies in "The Jonesci Charter", and give you a series of useful ideas or frameworks to help you implement your own **Jonesci Charter** in the most efficient way.

In doing so, I will share with you many of my experiences over the last 30+ years in business management, along with credit due to those places where I can remember picking up those that I didn't think of myself. In other words, I'm not about to re-invent the wheel when there are many masters that I can point you towards for particular aspects for further reference.

So where should we start to eliminate waste in our business... think of things that need to be done correctly every single time.

Any repetitive, routine work or where critical steps are completed. If you can focus on the Routine any exceptions can be managed by your team as you'll have sets of rules and options to guide them to make appropriate decisions and possibly implement additional systems to handle these variances.

Just remember... If there is anything you do without documenting it, you'll continue having to do it yourself until you do.

Now... it has been said that to have rigid systems in place will stifle creativity and lateral thinking in an organisation. Be aware that this can have an element of truth about it if you want this to happen, however, following the model in this book and encouraging or rewarding innovation for improving existing systems would actually reverse that potential.

It will also encourage more creativity as your team will be starting from a position of strength in having "a" system to follow rather than the state of confusion that surrounds having nothing in place.

But what if I am a one-man band – or employee?

Now, you'll note that my language in this book refers on the whole to working with your team, and developing systems for your team to use. So it's important for me to highlight here and now, that everything can apply to the "soloprenuer", those who work on their own, either in a business, or in a job. "Team" equally applies to all the Franchisees in the world who buy into and follow the Franchisor's systems also with their own team members. Every individual will operate at higher levels of best practice and operational efficiency where they have sound systems documented and easy to follow, learn and refer back to as needed.

The efficiency benefits still apply, and it makes it easier to get others to help out when you need it or are ready to branch out. The less the business is reliant upon the space between your ears having to remember everything, the more likely it is going to be able to thrive.

Also, if and when you decide to move on, up or out, it becomes a much more valuable asset to sell as the systems are already prepared and it is much easier for someone else to take over.

A dictionary definition of systems is.... *"a complex whole, a set of connected things or parts, an organized body of things"*.

It's all about creating a series of events or a structure to ensure there is consistency, efficiency and predictability with a higher level of reliability and speed. It sets a standard for "Best Practice" in productivity and reduced dependency on you with an easier reference point for initial and on-going training. In a nutshell, they can lead to you enjoying more time off!!

Sounds good doesn't it... but why isn't there a whole bunch of systems already written down to help make life easy... I guess at the end of the day there are so many different things that everyone does, and so many variations of each it would be a tall order to produce such a beast.

Chapter 1

Why do organisations waste so much time, energy and money?

This is the "show me the money chapter"... why would you go to the effort of creating a Jonesci Charter in your business, division or department.

The "Jonesci Charter" is a complete approach for anyone to follow – and adapt to your own style. It is not just about cutting expenses, but is a **"whole of business"** methodology to ensure a lean and agile operation that optimises it's opportunities. It includes all the elements you need to be effective, efficient and often effortless in your daily life.

Are you looking to make it easier to run your business or department? Do you want to take control and make it less reliant on you being there all the time?

You might be looking to capitalise on the value of the business when you sell it as part of your retirement plan.
Maybe you're thinking that you just can't find the right staff as no-one ever does it like you? Hmmm, how often have I heard that!!

How leaky is your bucket?

Let's explore some areas of your business or life that might be adversely affected right now, which could all be better handled by implementing some good systems into your business.

As you read through this over simplified starter list consider how each of these items or problems could be costing you in both Time and Money...and in business, time is money so **maybe even write it down in the margin to come back to later...**

Financial Issues...
- Lack of Cash-flow management
- Stock miss-management
- Minimal or poor tracking of costs and margins
- Waste not being measured
- Doing extras without charging clients – giving away your time
- Purchasing small, uneconomical quantities
- Not estimating quantities correctly and having to do last minute purchases from the local store
- Not knowing if hiring or buying would be cheaper
- Using estimates or guesses and not recording actual work time
- Accepting variation requests without costing them first and documenting

Time Management Skills
- Lack of task planning
- Poor delegation
- Not clear on priorities
- Too many interruptions
- Too many distractions
- Stress and tiredness from the overload
- Procrastination due to lack of knowledge or other fears
- Not measuring important behaviours

Operations / Quality Issues
- Re-doing incorrectly completed tasks
- No defined outcomes or targets
- Lack of consistency or routine
- Having to correct minor defects that slip through the cracks

- Not checking quality at completion of each stage of production or service delivery
- Not clarifying your expectation of job quality then having to re-do it.
- Constantly putting out spot fires

Lost Sales Opportunities...
- Not knowing what uniquely sets your business head and shoulders above the competition
- Poor sales conversion process – or lack of
- How to get clients to come back again
- Getting bigger sales from clients when they are buying
- Lack of, or in-consistent opportunity follow-ups
- Quotes that go nowhere

Ineffective Marketing Processes...
- Lack of persuasive, reliable and inexpensive ways to generate more leads or prospects
- No step-by-step marketing plan to significantly increase new business, consistently
- Spending on Marketing without measuring the return

Ineffective Communication
- Going to client or supplier visits only to find the key people were not there
- Poor communication of delays or changes in project timing
- Not confirming everyone's clear understanding when giving out instructions (then things go pear-shaped)
- Taking unnecessary phones calls from your team because they have nowhere else to refer to

Lack of Leadership Structure
- Lack of an organizational chart and position descriptions
- Procrastination through lack of a decision making process
- Sick of talk fests and anxious to start activity
- Meeting mania – pointless and ineffective meetings

Team Management Systems...
- Micro-Management of Others
- Poor delegation / Insufficient guidance or support
- Simple to produce and easy to understand reporting from your team/franchisees
- Understand process of how to lead rather than simply manage
- Ad-hoc recruiting not attracting the right team
- Lack of an ongoing training program to get the team to be more effective and more productive
- Not trained to deliver superior levels of customer service efficiently
- Poor use of time and working reactively, putting out fires

Planning / Preparation Systems...
- Team all seem so busy, but not getting the important things done
- Creating documents from scratch without using templates
- Scheduling or re-scheduling people and/ or tasks
- Unnecessary out of hours work / overtime
- Waiting for others to complete their tasks
- No clear or powerful personal or business goals detailed
- Lack of a clear vision for my company for everyone to aim for
- No action plan to keep us focused on what really is important

Restricted Exit or Expansion Strategies...
- No chance of taking regular holidays and trusting the business or your department will continue to run successfully
- No succession-plan to replace yourself with the right people to run it for you
- How to expand to multiple outlets or territories

- Need to create a franchise system that creates profitable franchisees
- Missing opportunities to take the company international

Each one of these challenges or frustrations is born from a lack of good systems. Inconsistency and mistakes come from flying blind and merely "hoping" that you and your team will do it the right way every time.

When working with clients I take them through a full 360 degree **"Leaky Bucket"** review of all areas of their business, to ensure each area is covered off properly with well documented systems in place and being followed.

Having been exposed to this so many times in the past, I consistently find that there are always areas to fine-tune or improve and each time, the investment of time is well rewarded once the strategies are built into the business systems.

Action Steps:
Using the lists in this chapter, take a moment now to write in here the main reasons for *you* for developing *your own* Jonesci Charter.

1. •

2. •

3. •

4. •

5. •

6. •

7. •

With your best estimate, what are the reasons listed above costing you in lost opportunity or time and actual cash wasted each and every year?

- Total _____

Does this hurt?

Chapter 2.

So...what Is "The Jonesci Charter"?

It's the 7 key elements to eliminating inefficiency and waste!

The "Jonesci Charter" is essentially an agreement – with yourself, your team, your board or your partners – to reduce the cost of doing business. In the word "cost" there are both Hard Costs and Soft Costs.

Hard Costs are those where you actually can see the "money in the bank" so to speak. They may come from re-negotiating supplier arrangements, selling off old stocks, reducing the labour overhead and so on.

Soft Costs are sometimes hard to quantify such is missed opportunities, or poor leadership, or lost clients due to unreliability.

Often I find these 2 types of costs will combine together for example where you know there is time wasted fixing up errors which could be quantified, but the value of the lost business due to the business or department not being able to work on future opportunities is difficult to quantify.

How should I use it?
- A "Jonesci Charter" can be just your own simple personal Charter for your role.

- You might be the leader of a department or small team and working with them to have a Team Charter would give everyone a tight focus to reducing inefficiencies and waste.

- Then of course the whole business should have it's own Global Charter encompassing all aspects of cost reduction to increase profits and success for everyone involved.

The Framework
In order to capitalise on the benefits available you need a framework to ensure it all comes together and the real benefits are achieved.

The "Jonesci Charter" is that framework. It has 7 key elements that when combined together will ensure you can enjoy the successes you are working so hard for.

The 7 Key Elements of your Jonesci Charter

Judgement
Listen, Observe, Analyse and Decide where inefficiencies are occurring. This is where we start to identify the best opportunities to eliminate inefficiency and wasted income.

Organisation
Organise who, where, what, when and why the system will be created. With a little bit of preparation you can gain a lot of traction towards your desired goals.

Numbers

You have to know your numbers. There are critical drivers in all roles and they need to be measured. Some numbers are easy to measure, others more difficult, so we'll explore the best options.

Efficacy

This is the power to produce the desired result. Is your team fully empowered? There are considerable Leadership skills involved in any Charter so here is where we cover off on what is needed.

Systemology

The Systems, Frameworks, Methods that are needed, all readily available and understandable for others to refer to, and get trained on. What is missing and how do you get this done.

Collaboration

Where can you work with others to get leverage and efficiencies. A major part of your Charter in today's competitive world is to establish a strong sense of collaboration both internally and externally.

Innovation

New thinking and changing paradigms are a real fact of life that can either help you or eat you up. Are you up to date with the current innovations available to you? What are you doing to develop your own Constant and Never Ending Improvement?

Your Charter Is Your Mantra

In the next 7 chapters I will explain how to implement each of these 7 key elements of your Jonesci Charter.

Look at your Charter as a long term and ongoing project, of constant and never-ending improvement to develop what I call the 5 Key Pro's of business….

Each of these Pro's run through each element of the Charter structure, and each area of business for you to be competing at your best level.

The 5 Core Pro's for Plain Sailing:
1. Productivity
2. Proficiency
3. Profitability
4. Process
5. Proof

The glue that holds all this together is of course Process or Procedure. It ties each one together to great effect.

Without Procedures, Productivity is gone due to inconsistencies, errors, procrastination…need I go on.

Without Procedures your Proficiency is undermined due to inconsistencies, errors and procrastination.

Without checking in to "Prove" it is all working according to plan on a regular basis, which requires it to be part of the Process, again you'll be slow to learn when things are notbeing done properly.

Hmmm? So do you think Profitability is affected in the same way? I know it is which is why I am so strong on their need. Without them there is a lot wasted. We'll cover that more in the Systemology chapter.

Action Steps:

Before reading ahead though...take a moment now to write in here 5 areas of waste repeated frequently by you or your team that perhaps maybe, perhaps could, just be eliminated.

1. •

2. •

3. •

4. •

5. •

'Systemise the routine, Humanise the exceptions'.

Chapter 3

Judgement

Listen > Observe > Analyse > Decide!

Are you inquisitive? How often do you challenge the status quo?

There is excess everywhere. Only when things are tough do I find a focus on saving money...which is not necessarily the right approach.

The majority of the money I have put back into the profitability of the businesses I have worked with has been low hanging fruit simply because no-one has questioned it previously. Or perhaps, if they had questioned it, there was either a lack of time or ability to do anything about it. Now I put that down to what I call "poor priority management" – in other words – too busy doing other things that are lower priorities.

I've always been a listener and observer. You know, one of those quiet types who'll sit in a meting and not say a lot, maybe asking a few pertinent questions trying to uncover the real meat. You might not be surprised that in doing this I find some great solutions simply by listening and observing.

I have a chuckle when I hear the analogy of giving a consultant your watch so he can tell you the time...but there is so much of a need for that simply because we are often too close to things ourselves to see "the time". It takes someone with a focus, to actually cut through the noise and find the gold.

I like to ask "why?" Why do we do this? Why don't you do that? Why is that happening? But then you need to listen for the answers with full focus. Listening simply to fill the next silence with another question or statement is not going to get you far.

The first response is so often only the scratch on the surface and you'll need to dig deeper with more probing questions.

The whole reason for developing your own "Jonesci Charter" is to create that "priority". It is needed as a part of the culture of the organisation. With no Charter there will only be minimal focus on inefficiency and waste as the main focus in any organisation is growth – Marketing, Sales, Business Development, Customer Relations…they all get the big budget, the time and energy, and perhaps quite rightly so as growth is important when done correctly.

There does however need to be a balance – counter-balance if you like to ensure that this growth is capitalised on at the optimum levels. I often question why some areas of an organisation actually exist – are they making there own contribution to the profits or is there a better way? Are these products really benefitting the business or does the extra support required eat up all the profit margins they might have.

So where to start?

I like to get some quick wins on the board first to ensure momentum is gained and maybe any budget required for future improvements has started being created. I am looking for things like bottlenecks causing delays or other inefficiencies as band-aid solutions.

I am looking for excesses in spend with little or no return. I am looking for out of control, maverick or ad-hoc spending. Another I love is "we've always done it that way" when so often there is now a better way.

My 5 quick and easy favourites are…
- to create a MindMap
- to do a SWOT analysis,
- a Survey to ask for External or Internal Feedback,
- to review relevant reports to highlight potential,
- and to dig into who does what and why.

The Leaky Bucket Challenge
A 6th and more detailed is my "Leaky Bucket" challenge in which I take you through an intensive "leak plugging" process over a period of one month to establish where the time should be best spent and an action plan to start plugging them. More details on this at the back of this book but it has enabled $Millions to be saved from leaking.

Mind Maps
I have found 9 key branches cover the sources of most leaks and grouping them like this makes it easier to organise and make progress.

The MindMap below is a starter and thought prompter for you to expand upon with more "limbs".

Some of these areas may well be strengths in your organisation which is fabulous...the others will be letting the side down...also in the spirit of constant improvement even those strengths could still be "leaking" and it is the 1% improvement here and there that combines to make significant improvements in your bottom line.

Highlight or colour code each limb or branch traffic light style in red, amber and green showing the priority or significance of each potential for leakage. This is highly visual and free thinking allowing random ideas to be captured and grouped appropriately.

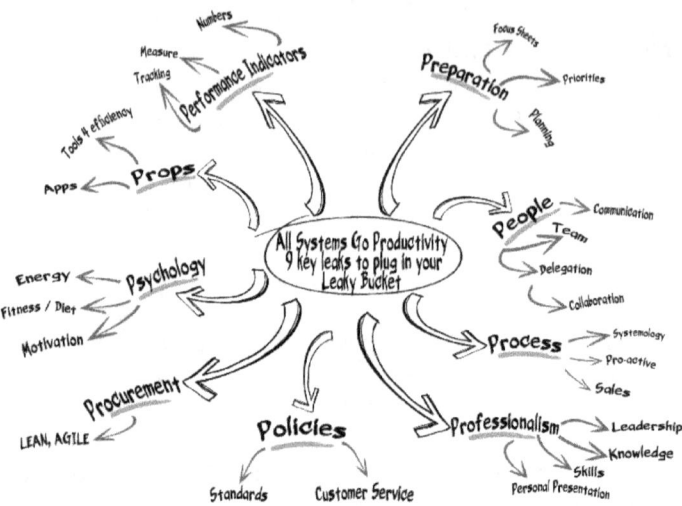

Surveys
A Survey can be done in any number of ways, as I am sure you are aware. It can be a simple set of questions asked verbally to relevant individuals...one by one or in a group. It could be a more detailed questionnaire sent out for replying to in writing by a certain deadline. Or as we are talking efficiency perhaps the initial approach should be by using an on-line questioning system that will even collate the responses for you into a simple report.

These surveys again can be internally within your team, as well as externally to suppliers and clients as well as others who know your business who are willing to help out as they have a vested interest.

SWOT Analysis
A SWOT analysis is often done at the higher management level – but is equally effective at shop floor level too. So often there is pure gold waiting to be tapped in to from our team members if only we would listen. In doing a S.W.O.T analysis we are looking at Strengths, Weaknesses, Opportunities and Threats.

This is often drawn up in a square grid but doesn't have to be. The key thing to take on when doing a SWOT is to understand that every comment, or thought has potential and should be noted, regardless of how ridiculous it may seem at the time.

Strengths and Weaknesses are deemed to be "Internal" or more under your own direct control.
Opportunities and Threats are deemed to be "External" and influences such as the environment, government decisions and other things out of your direct control.

A kick start for you would be to break down your SWOT against the 9 key areas for Leakages, in the form of a MindMap as mentioned earlier. This is excellent, both as a team but also on an individual level. Simply by adding another branch for each key you will start to uncover some exciting opportunities to improve or capitalise upon.

Reports
Reports can often be a good starting point for identifying issues of waste or inefficiency, and then may need further digging into the data behind the reports to ascertain the knowledge needed to continue.

One that I have used to huge effect in the past is the standard Income and Expenditure reporting especially where it can be broken down into line details. I look for expense items that have not been analysed or reviewed for some time (often years) and then dig deeper from there.

As far as digging into who does what and why, this is designed to uncover tasks that higher paid staff are doing when technology or lower paid teams members should be doing them. This is often part of my Priority Management training when busy professionals and executives suddenly realise they can be much more effective at what they are paid to do. When figuring out where to start improving, ask yourself...

- Identify what your hourly rate should be if you were charging a client for your real value.
- Consider what jobs you are doing that you could pay someone a lot less to do for you. Especially identify the jobs that you are doing on a regular basis.
- Are there any jobs which you really don't enjoy doing?
- Pick one to start the ball rolling.

The Decision

Having done a considerable amount of Listening, Observing and Analysis...some items will undoubtedly jump off the page at you and scream... fix me and you'll be laughing. Sure enough you could generate some big wins fairly quickly and think that's all you need to do, but be warned that *this will be like giving the old girl just another lick of paint...*

You need to address the foundations too and by installing the complete package and systemising the whole business your team will embrace a different culture ensuring that benefits are maintained long term.

The break-even point is always a key consideration in the decision process. While things could be improved, maybe an investment of time or money is required to make the improvement. Is that investment worth while? Is the return guaranteed or what is the likelihood of getting a good return? What is the time frame involved and can we cash-flow it during that time?

I always like to use systems to improve profitability, and start off by looking for areas of inefficiency. The results of inefficiency always boil down to 3 key areas, time, cost and quality.

The inevitable result of mismanagement of each of these is lower profits. Identify a level of inefficiency in each case, including time and quality, and you can quickly estimate the hard cost financially to your business through a lack of a good system.

By estimating the cost in hours, or dollars in each of the many areas of business that are typically running inefficiently, you can quickly extrapolate those numbers out to determine what this could be costing you annually. This often includes too many zeros at the end of the number.

The results of these calculations may cause you concern when you realise how big some of these numbers are. However, they could equally cause you great excitement when you realise that by a simple process of systemisation, you could make a huge impact on your time management and profitability.

The doubters among us will want to re-calculate the numbers. Whichever way you look at it, the numbers tell you a story and I urge you to get started somewhere without delay. Procrastination is one of the biggest thieves to your success and it is your choice to stop that happening.

You might be spending too much time micro managing your team, fixing up errors or re-inventing the wheel each time a task is performed. You might be paying staff for too much un-billable time, managing your stock poorly, or not estimating jobs properly which can all cost unnecessarily. Quality issues may be due to faults getting through to the final stage of production before being identified, warranty re-works, or ineffective training.

These are only a handful of examples and the list is long, each potentially costing your business thousands of dollars which could be added to your profits with the production and following of some simple systems.

Action Steps:

Take the time now to start a thorough SWOT Mind Map based on the example provided. Highlight the S.W.O.T for each of the 9 key limbs, Preparation, People, Process, Professionalism, Props, Procurement, Psychology, Performance Indicators and Policies.

Chapter 4

Organisation

Begin with the end in mind.

Ok, so that's a bit of an easy statement to make, but when there are many different issues to benefit from – you have to ask – "how do I know what to work on first?"

When heading off on a long voyage, we need to have a plan. Where are we going and what do we need to consider as variables along the way.

Of course, as with doing anything properly, you need to plan...

"fail to plan, or plan to fail... your choice!"

Plenty has been written before about Planning so what I want to cover off here are a few fundamentals to your Jonesci Charter.

We know that we need Goals in our striving for success and your Charter is no exception. Before re-inventing the wheel...what is your company Vision and Mission Statement. Does it have any focus at all on being a Lean and Agile organisation minimising inefficiency and unnecessary expenditure? If not then maybe it needs a slight tweak.

Once our Vision and Mission is clear and known by the whole team.. that is a first and major step in the equation. The company will need more specific time-framed goals to start driving the process, then each individual, or department can add their own goals to contribute to the Charter. The power is when everyone is working together towards a strong Vision.

You'll need to consider a number of different ways of implementing the Charter... My favourite is to have a senior team member as the Champion to carry it forward. Someone who has a passion for making this happen. That person may also be someone who loves to play with numbers and show profit improvements. They will need to have the trust and respect of the team to be open and supportive.

Then there will be the need to allocate time where appropriate to efficiently get the results being sought. This time can easily be justified though once you have been through Stage 1 – Judgement, and realised how much value there is to you to gain from investing this time.

More often than not though – this time can be "free" due to the spare capacity in some team members – I can actually say from my Coaching experience that "some" should in fact read as "most" team members – so it is more of a case of priority management and not time management.

Mind-Mapping

You'll find I'm a fan of what I call mudmaps (known properly as "Mindmaps"). A Mindmap enables you to just throw your thoughts randomly on to paper, or a computer, pulling them into some kind of order as you go, but without getting too bogged down, or distracted by the detail. You'll have seen an example in the "J" chapter earlier in this book.

Here is a mind map for part of the Marketing area for a Promotion Products business.

Work with your team to develop a mind map for each area or department of your business that can generate improvements.

At this stage it does not need to be recorded to the smallest of details... big chunks now, then fill in the gaps later!

Start by creating a new mind map for your business and create four branches (virtually any business will use these four main areas):

- Marketing

- Sales

- Operations – Service or Product Delivery

- Administration/Management

Make sure you have listed all the key opportunities within the area you are working on that were identified in Step 1 – Judgement.

Add any missing opportunities or newly identified ones to the relevant area of the mind map you are working on and reword if necessary.

Project Planning

Once you have your Plan established for starting – there are other things to ensure become included so a collaborative Project Management tool would be beneficial.

Rate the Importance

Mark against each task the importance of it to the business. This might be High, Medium, or Low or another scale you choose to make up yourself. Must Do, Should Do, and Could Do is another possibility.

Who is Responsible

Indicate who is responsible for performing this task. Highlight the key stakeholders and who this task affects both upstream and downstream. Who performs tasks immediately prior to this task that might be affected, and who immediately afterwards that will be affected. Relevant parties need to get feedback and consult with these people to ensure the result is an efficient and effective system for everyone.

Sign off

Does anyone else need to ensure that this task has been completed. Does an owner or manager need to have sign off.

Will it require a checklist

Mark which tasks require a checklist, or to be part of another checklist to ensure they are done.

Identify and record the stakeholders for each project

When working on process improvement include:
- The **Process Owner** – this is the person who knows the most about the process – most likely the person doing it

- The **Process Team** – these are the other team members directly involved with the process

    o Team members who work in the process that comes **directly before** the process/area you're working on

    o Team members who work in the process that comes **directly after** the process you're working on

- **Other Stakeholders** – those that can contribute to the outcome but have a less direct role in the process. These could also be people upstream or downstream from that process.

How to set some goals

You want this process to focus on what's most cost effective for the business.

You'll want complete participation and buy in from the team on the final product. The key stakeholders need to meet and set the priorities and set some goals.

A widely accepted rule to follow to gauge whether or not your goals are well written is to follow the process of writing **S.M.A.R.T** (Specific, Measurable, Achievable, Results Focussed, and Time-framed) goals. If your goals don't meet each of these criteria then they need more attention to ensure they are goals that can work for you.

It is advisable to choose to include team members in setting these goals as well. Your strategic management can't dictate what is right from the top if there is significant divergence here (and there frequently is in medium sized businesses where the owner or management is less involved in day-to-day operations).

You will want any training in the future to be in line with any new systems created.

This will require that everyone has a clear and positive understanding throughout the organization that the Charter is dynamic and living – "this is how we do it now, but if the business changes or if someone comes up with a better way, we will change".

The whole company needs to come away with a commitment and a plan for continuous self-audit using KPIs and reviews to make sure that the organisation is operating the way it should optimally and to evaluate and incorporate any innovations that surface in the future.

Action Steps:
Get yourself a Mind-mapping tool and practice by mapping out the key areas in your business as I have described. Then in each area, highlight the key areas that could provide you some quick wins! Maybe jot them down here until you are in front of a computer.

1. •

2. •

3. •

"A system will work only when it is easier to use the system than ignore it"

Chapter 5

Numbers

If it can be quantified – measure it.

All areas of business need to have some kind of measurement to gauge performance. Sometimes the measurement is a basic and easily known number while others may need a bit more forethought into how best to establish a benchmark. Often a higher-level measurement is easier to track and keep an eye on and then occasionally you'll need to dig deeper into what causes it to pinpoint opportunities to improve.

Let's explore some ways that we can keep a measurement in areas of business that are key to our success.

In his book "Keeping Score", Mark Brown advocates that measurements should focus on the past, present, and future and be based on the needs of the customers, shareholders, *and* employees. Measuring everything is however more damaging than measuring nothing so pinpointing the vital measures is the key to success.

He explains there are two approaches – "top down" where corporate executives exert control…this is usually faster to implement and with less inconsistencies – the second approach being by unit or location where business units or locations have greater autonomy.

So what is measured by successful organisations… and where should you start? Start with a short-list (perhaps not-so-short) of examples. The list below is a starting point… this will have you thinking along the right lines for your business or department to manage expenditure and reduce inefficiencies. This list is by no means exhaustive and, depending on your business, there will be more or better options.

Corporate / Financial Measures
- Return on equity, Return on Investment
- Earnings growth
- Margins / Mark ups - % and $
- Percentage earnings growth
- Dollar profit before taxes
- Dollar net income
- Debtors, Creditors
- Stock Levels
- Breakeven Point
- Actuals vs Budget
- Bad Debts
- Real Discounts Given
- Inventory levels

Sales & Marketing
- Percentage sales growth per year
- Lead Sources & No of Leads from each
- Conversion rates
  - overall for all business
  - by product/service
  - at stage of cycle
- Dollar Total Sales
- Percentage Sales by Product or Region
- Average Sale Value
  - Overall for the business
  - By Marketing Strategy
- Acquisition Cost

Employees
- Wages as % of turnover – by location/department
- Overtime Cost
- Employee satisfaction index
- Training hours per employee
- Diversity percentages

- Performance vs. objectives – plans
- Employee turnover % or number
- Billable Hours
- Absenteeism
- Lost time due to injury / Compensation Claims

Customers
- Customer satisfaction index
- Complaints/shipments
- Flawless execution index
- Percentage market share
- Repeat Business
- Client Retention (time)
- Lifetime Value (Total Sales Margin)

Technology
- Percentage sales from new products
- Technical service customer satisfaction levels
- Subscriptions usage

Productivity
- Cost per unit
- Capacity Utilisation
- Dollar profit per employee
- Warranty Claims
- Re-works – before and after delivery
- Part / Incorrect Shipments / Back Orders
- Time spent doing certain tasks
- Downtime

Speed
- On-time delivery - number or %
- Days to resolve complaints
- Cycle time – product development / response
- Duplication of tasks / time taken to complete

Responsibility or Care Metrics
- Compliance with responsible care codes

- Lost-time incident rate
- Percentage reduction of emissions
- Percentage total waste reduction

Supply Chain
- Purchasing expenditure
- Cost comparisons to marketplace
- On-time deliveries
- Number of unique suppliers
- Monthly contracts
- Supplier errors / defects
- Incorrect / Part Shipments
- Time since last review
- Credit terms

Now you are probably wondering what some of these prompters have to do with reducing waste or inefficiencies and quite reasonably so.

The simple explanation is they all have an impact on or are a reflection of the organisation's profitability, so therefore can tell us where to look to make improvements. For example the Sales metrics can indicate inefficient sales processes, which might be due to a systems issue, or a training or staff turnover issue.

More often than not the initial process of Judgement or "Justification" by way of SWOT or other reviews, will highlight areas that are thought to be inefficient or wasteful and it is often then necessary to establish proof or measurement of the current status quo in order to make better decisions going forward. One of these decisions might then be made… it's not that bad and better gains can be made by applying our resources elsewhere, or indeed it might scream, let's get on with this and do something about it – the measurement then being a useful indicator afterwards as to the level of success achieved.

A question I like to ask is "What would you need to know if you were away on vacation for 3 months to know your company is operating well without you?". Can you boil the key measurements down to a 1-page summary, for your department – or the whole business?

Comparing figures from one month to the next, or to the same month last year, will highlight variances that you'll want to dig into more deeply.

Cost Reduction Reviews

For five years I made a pretty decent income by analysing and re-organising company expenditure on a line item basis. I was that confident of achieving a result I worked on a success fee basis, being paid a percentage of the first year's savings identified.

I regularly reviewed simple things like Stationery, Telephone Bills, plus a wide variety of Raw Materials, other Overhead expenses such as Truck tyres and Canteen expenses and there was always some very low hanging fruit. Many of the reviews achieved over $100,000 of annualised savings per expense. In some cases errors were found resulting in 2-3 years of refunds being clawed back by clients due to over-charging of their suppliers.

Now due to the fact that I really had to justify my claim at the end, I put an unduly large amount of extra time into getting exact figures of the current expenditure, which was a little counter-productive for me, but my clients were always happy. Imagine doing this for yourself, you wouldn't need to go to that in-depth detail just for "proof" so should get the exercise done a whole lot quicker.

Knowing Your Costs

Do you really know how much things cost you? More than likely, everything will cost more than you expect. If you manufacture do you know how much it costs to produce a particular product? Similarly, operating a service has costs that you most likely don't measure...or even consider.

Many of your expenses are never evaluated. If you take some time to find out what your actual costs are you can then look at ways of reducing them if it is worth the time doing it.

By getting quotes on different services and products you can save substantial amounts of money. There's nothing wrong with shopping around and finding a better deal on everything – you'll find one.

As a manufacturer the only way to accurately determine the cost of a particular product is to measure it. This should be done at regular intervals as over time cost will change. Depending on the business this could be done once a week, month, quarter or at the worst once a year. If you wrongly assume that costs have remained stationary and costs have increased, you could get into trouble very quickly.

When measuring the costs it is important to understand that there are two different costs to be considered **Direct** and **Indirect** costs.

Direct Costs

Direct costs are the easiest to understand as these are the costs directly associated with doing a particular job. The most common categories consist of Raw Materials Used, Hours Worked, Hire of Equipment, Sub Contractors, Delivery and Consumables.

One of the best ways to measure your direct costs is to use a pre printed cost sheet which follows the job as it goes through the production process and all costs are recorded.

Indirect Costs

Just by opening your doors you incur costs whether you have a job to do or not. Rent, electricity, gas, phone, insurance, interest, and administration must all be paid regardless. In addition wages and costs that are not directly associated with production such as Sales and Administration need to be accounted for. An **Overhead** is the indirect cost of doing business and it needs to be included in the costing of products and of doing business.

One simple method for allocating Overhead is to total up the overhead costs for the year/quarter/month and divide it by the number of production hours for the year/quarter/month. This will give you an average $ per production hour. This can be applied to the costing of a particular product based on the number of production hours used to produce that product. This is important consideration when trying to ensure you are focussing on the right parts of your business when making sales.

Data Collection Instruments and Procedures

This is the part that will take the most time with costs sometimes attached to outside resources. Determine which you can do internally and which is better done externally.

Prepare a data collection instruments and procedures Matrix. For each category determine if the data exists (yes, no), use as is (yes/no), make/buy (N/A, buy, make) and project manager (who is responsible). Then develop a timeline for the completion of the project.

Daily Personal Productivity

A tricky thing to actually measure, but a tool that I have created and used very effectively myself, and with clients and colleagues is what I call "SAM" or "Success Action Matrix".

This is ideally suited to those who are free to make up their own agenda for the majority of each day, so can be prone to do what they choose, or what is urgent, instead of what is important. By writing up a list of Must Do and Should Do tasks and rating them on a weighting scale of 1 to 10 in points for their level of importance (not urgency). This value should then be divided by the number of times that could be done in a standard unit of time such as one hour, to give it a value. Lets say in a Management role, team meetings were important and would score 5 points for a 30min meeting. You might score only 7 points for a one-hour meeting in order to encourage efficient meetings that don't linger unnecessarily. Another important task might be contacting suppliers or clients to set up a meeting with them. Maybe 10 calls could be completed in one hour so each call would be worth 1 point. Each of your major priorities can be broken down into smaller chunks as they often are in reality, and allocated their "weighting" scores.

By keeping a simple score sheet on your desktop, or tablet, by the end of each day you'll have a score for the day. You'll be surprised at how well this process keeps you focussed on the priorities of your role…and then how effective you become. Your competitive nature can kick in too and motivate you daily to beat your best.

Action Steps:
1. Write up your own S.A.M and start focussing on your priorities.
2. Identify the numbers you need to measure regularly.

Chapter 6

Efficacy

The Power To Produce The Desired Result

The dictionary definition of Efficacy is "The Power to produce the desired result" and that effectively comes from quality Leadership.

For your Jonesci Charter to work – you need to empower those responsible to make it happen. Simple! It cannot just be a motherhood statement, but everyone to own it, understand it, and support it, so this always starts with quality leadership.

With quality leadership, you have Efficacy. Efficacy will provide strong change management abilities too and, as is often the way with setting goals to make improvements, there will be roadblocks in your path ahead to navigate. We aim to make these as small as possible.

My 18 keys of Leadership

There are many, many good books and specialists on Leadership so I am not going to spend a lot of time here with profound Leadership training... but simply highlight in bullet point fashion the Leadership traits which I believe are necessary for your Charter to be effective.

1. Talks About The Future
- Leaders think about the future and help others see the future. *"Leaders teach people to dream, not just execute".*
- Enrol your team in the big picture, giving them a clear mental picture of the reality they want to create.
- Compare the future with the present.

- Leadership is not position, it is action. Leaders take action in the moment to create the future... continuously.
- As their leader you'll be talking about the benefits of the "Jonesci Charter" and operating a Lean and Agile operation.
- Communication is the oil that keeps the machine working – use good oil.

2. Forward Planning
- Think of what will or may happen down the road,
- Think of trends, where are markets going, think in terms of value migration... what will customers want in the future and how you can be efficient and effective as an organisation to adapt ahead of the trend.
- Create the future. Think about changes in health, key people, technology problems in the future. Think of scenarios in the future that your organisation could capitalise on.
- You need to plan ahead, write them down and act on them.
- Be prepared!

3. Developing Others
- Leaders are involved in their organisation and committed to growing organisational capability and efficiency.
- Nothing sends that signal stronger than taking a moment to teach someone something.
- Encourage the building of knowledge and skills through training both internally and externally.
- Enables more leverage of your time as your team around you grows stronger.
- Learn to help people with more than just their jobs: help them with their lives

4. Constantly Learning
- Build your Knowledge every day.
- Build on your Experiences.

- Encourage Team for Seeking Improvement.
- Actively look for ideas and then champion them in your organisation.
- Accept change as a leader.

5. Give Recognition
- Builds not only enthusiasm for the work, but trust in management.
- Tell someone they did a "good job".
- Hand out praise when a job, large or small, is well done.
- Help those who are doing poorly to do well, and help those who are doing well to do even better.
- Your candle loses nothing when it lights another.

6. Get Mad – Then Get Over It
- Leaders all have passion for the business and sometimes this passion turns to anger or frustration.
- This shows you are only human.
- An effective leader has the capacity to move beyond emotion into constructive action.
- Let it go... don't dwell on it.
- Make the point clear, and fair. No Insults.
- True communication is the response you get!

7. Mix In The Right Circles
- Collaboration is crucial nowadays.
- Know which relationships are key to your success.
- Meet someone new in your circle of influence.
- Get out and say "hello," to someone new in or near your business.
- It's guaranteed that you will learn something and it is visible proof to your organisation that you care.
- Where best can you get the quality support you need to be as efficient and effective as possible.

8. Be Enthusiastic
- Leaders have enthusiasm and energy.

- They transfer this energy to the organisation and the business issues at hand.
- Practice being outright enthusiastic about an idea and watch how people change.
- Keep your energy up... eat and sleep well.

9. Be Decisive
- Eliminate Procrastination.
- Find something where you can say "yes." Nothing says you trust your organisation more than the power of agreement.
- Use Initiative.
- A Crisis is inevitable and is your chance to perform. Deal with it straightforwardly and head-on and straight away.
- Act courageously when courage is called for.
- Make a commitment - One person with courage is a majority

10. Actively Listen
- Two eyes, two ears and one mouth, use them in that proportion.
- Many of us talk about being good listeners, but few of us are really good at it.
- The next time you are asked to listen to someone, use clarifying and confirming skills, but don't offer a point of view until they ask
- Ask and Listen for individual Motivators – they are normally about Career, Money, Personal Growth, or doing Something Meaningful
- Great for conflict resolution skills.
- To connect with their hearts, use your ears;

11. Be Positive
- Also practise the quality of responsible optimism.
- Managers help people see themselves as they are; Leaders help people to see themselves better than they are.
- Be approachable, fair & considerate

- Lead by example
- Eliminate negative from your life

12. Practice Impeccable Integrity
- Integrity is the basis of trust.
- Make a decision based on integrity, on your sense of values…and *Know What Your Values Really Are!*
- The value of a promise is the cost of keeping it, so make promises carefully.
- A promise to yourself, which no one else knows about, if broken, diminishes your self-esteem.
- Be True to Yourself

13. Take Responsibility
- When placed in charge – take command
- Be responsible for everything that you are.
- "The buck stops with you".
- Refuse to make excuses, blame or criticise anyone else.
- Immediately resolve to fix the situation…. Step out & take charge.
- If you are constructive and helpful, people will look to you for solutions in a crisis. Be a Piece of the Rock;
- If you can't carry the ball, you can't lead the Team;

14: Avoid Temptations
- Ego…
- Abuse Of Authority/Power…
- Lack of Accountability…
- Earn, don't command respect;
- Needing to be 100% Certain…
- Desire for Harmony
- Fear of Vulnerability – Trusting Others
- Leaders don't need to be liked, they need to be respected'

15: Be Disciplined and Organised
- Do whatever it takes…get external discipline if needed
- Great organisational skills…

- Impeccable Time Management…
- Choose Your Pain…
  - *Discipline* – This is the pain <u>now</u> – Do whatever it takes;
  - *Regret* – This pain comes <u>later</u> and you cant change the past.
  - <u>Discipline</u> weighs ounces while <u>Regret</u> weighs tons.

16: Excellent Delegation
- You can't do it all - Learn to let go;
- Not abdication – delegate properly
- Review tasks required to achieve he Jonesci Charter aims and either Delete, Delegate, Systematize or Outsource;
- Have systems in place so you can delegate and you don't have to do everything yourself;
- Ensure the time, resources, tools and budget is available in order to not undermine their attempts
- Manage resources, lead people

17: Measure Your Progress
- As in the previous chapter – know your numbers
- Have SMART Goals (Specific, Measureable, Achievable, Result Focussed, Time-framed)
- Know Your Key Performance Indicators (KPI's)
- Over ambitious targets can be a de-motivator as you and your team become defeated
- Measure Activity That Leads To Positive Outcomes
- Keep Yourself and Others Accountable
- Understand What Your Measurements Highlight

18. Have Fun
- Leaders typically enjoy what they are doing, no matter how tough the task.
- People want to follow someone who enjoys what they are doing.
- The first impression can seal the deal.
- Encourage your team to enjoy themselves.

- Be spontaneous
- Smiles Are Infectious

An exercise I like to do when working with clients on their Leadership is to have them do a quick self-score on each of these characteristics so they can start to identify areas to build on. Rate each item out of 10, being honest with yourself.

Obviously this is a subjective approach but always highlights good starting points.

Getting peers to rate you too adds another dimension completely.

Try it yourself.

How well did you score?

What areas can you start to improve this week, and then add to over the next few weeks?

Action Steps:
Take a few moments to list out any potential roadblocks that you need to address.

1. •

2. •

3. •

4. •

5. •

6. •

7. •

Chapter 7

Systemology

Create consistency With Properly Constructed Frameworks

Consider this...

…. It's 9am tomorrow morning and the phone rings... it is one of your key employees with some bad news... for you, at least. They have just been notified of an inheritance and won't be in today... or tomorrow, in fact never again. It's about now that you realise there are a whole stack of things that need to be done, and all the information is in this employee's head... no-one else knows how to do the job, and nothing is written down for someone to try to pick up and run with.

Now there are a number of similar stories with a potentially similar outcome, ...they have a terminal illness, or they've won the lottery, got a new job... or any other of a number of reasons... fact is, they are not there to tell you how they did their job... and it's too late to get the steps written down by them now.

Here's something else to think about...
You are a prisoner in your own business. When was the last time you got a decent break away from it yet it still continued to operate and generate a profit. Why is that?

It can be said that to do a repetitive task without documenting the process, will mean that you are destined to repeat that task yourself forever if you want it done the same way. The first step in leveraging yourself more time and control, is to step by step record how things should be done, and clearly so that others can do them for you.

Many of you will read that statement and think... how in the world am I going to find time to do all that. Yes, it could be a little bit of a task, but the more important thing to work out first is to ask yourself...

> "what is our inefficiency really costing me?"...

If you take the time to think about it, the answer will certainly motivate you into action. If that's not enough, then consider the scenarios I opened this book with and ask yourself...

> "what could my lack of systems really cost me?"...

As I explained in the intro, by creating effective systems, things work better and you don't waste time fixing things up or having to re-do work at further expense to your business. Effective systems will save you and your team both time and money.

Highly successful Dentist and author of "The Happiness Centred Business" Paddi Lund tells how he has used systems in his practice to..

> "...make difficult things easier to do".

He also says that...

> "systems make it possible for us to free our brains while we perform habitual tasks"

Have you ever tried to do Rubic's Cube?

If you are like me, and failed, it was most likely that you were taking a random approach to it.
I remember a friend of my daughters teaching her how she

follows a simple system to solve Rubic's Cube in a very short space of time. (Though I must admit that is NOT a system that I have chosen to master yet).

In effect, once the process has been thought through, and tested, our minds are then free to be more creative, and able to do other things like communicating on a higher level with our clients, whilst performing the routine which has become habit.

"But"... people have said to me... "*my business is different*".... or... "*there are too many variations of what we do*". When digging only a little deeper I find that there are a vast number of similarities to other business operations, so I suggest you start somewhere. For example... the basic rule for systemizing your business according to Mike Basch – founder of Federal Express is...

'Systemise the routine, Humanise the exceptions'.

Don't worry about the complicated bits to start with, just focus on the routine stuff which you'll usually find boils down to Pareto's 80:20 rule allowing you to cover the bulk of your work without to many complications.

Anything that cannot be automated using technology needs to be run by people. People-run systems are those repeatable processes and procedures that produce tangible results and quality outcomes for the business.

Always look at putting a system in place rather than employing more people. A system means that things are done consistently, "by-the-numbers", regardless of which team member actually performs the task. Einstein said that...

"Insanity is doing the same thing over and over again, expecting different results".

Happily, from a business owner's perspective,

"Sanity is doing the same thing over and over again, expecting the same or better results".

Why? Consistency and continuous improvement can only be achieved if there is a base to start from. Putting systems in place creates the opportunity for improvement and ultimately provides the only chance to achieve true excellence!

Our clients want consistency...

As the Business Owner or Manager you want... the right people, doing the right thing, the right way, and at the right time.
- ✓ *Systems* should run your business consistently and reliably...
- ✓ The right *People* will run your systems and work to improve them...
- ✓ *Your* role is to lead your people to take ownership of their roles...

The well worn comparison is made over and over again...

"Why is it that McDonalds and other successful Business can all manage to present the same levels of service and quality consistently...with a bunch of teenagers who you can't get to do even the simplest of tasks at home?"

The answer, of course, is that they have well proven systems that everyone is trained to follow... then the youngsters they employ simply turn up at work and follow the system.

While creating systems can seem to be a tedious project to take on... the results show certainly better consistency, and whilst they don't guarantee 100% compliance and your team could divert from following a system, they wouldn't be able to use the old chestnut of an excuse... "I wasn't sure what to do".

.... but where do I start..?

LOGIC & PROFIT

In my book "Systemology" I explain in more detail how to create actual systems using the LOGIC model and where you need to make adjustments – the PROFIT model. I'll cover the basics here to get you started.

This is where you get into the detail and record your systems. This can be done in many different ways and you'll need to decide what works best for you.

I'll start by asking you to consider whether you think your team would want to read a long descriptive process to learn a system.

Whilst there are occasions where this is important and necessary, typically I find that most would prefer to either watch a video or look at a flowchart for its more visual representation making it a simple thing to follow. Sometimes a simple series of pictures can help paint the picture. Whichever you use, you'll be one step ahead of those who do nothing.

Break it into Big Chunks

First thing to make life easy, is to map out the main steps in the process that you might look at as the over simplified system.

The 1 – 10 – 5 System

Yes, I can count. A colleague of mine introduced me to a simple way of chunking, essentially laying out the beginning, the end, and then the middle. So 1 – 10 – 5 refers to Step 1, Step 10, and Step 5....

It really doesn't matter how many steps there are and you can pick your own numbers, you might choose 1 - 8 - 4 or any other sequence for that matter.... The essence being... **beginning, end and then the middle.**

Let's Have A Go.

For Example - Making a Cup of Coffee

If I was to suggest you write a system to make a cup of coffee, the simple system you come up with might just be...

1. Boil the kettle
2. Put coffee in cup
3. Add boiling water
4. Add milk and sugar

Sounds pretty logical for most of us – but then others might say – "not enough information".

Just by reading these 4 steps you might be thinking things like, is there water in the kettle, how much coffee, is it instant or ground, or de-caf, how much milk, who said I wanted sugar, etc, highlighting that even for a simple task like this, there are quite a few variables and options that can and will make a difference. So we need to be clear in our instructions.

Map the Process – Flowcharting the Steps

Having identified the high value areas of the business start with one of these. Gather together all the stakeholders involved in this process.

Clearly set out the objectives for the session, allocate roles for the session, be clear that everyone is there to actively participate and make sure everyone knows why they have been included in the session.

Be clear on what a successful end result will be for the session. Remember, do not get bogged down on the detail, just get something down and then refine it later.

Consider what does go wrong with the process you are working on at the moment, think about what can go wrong and what is working well.

Fill in the details...

By flowcharting your processes, starting with the big chunks, you'll find it easier to add in all the smaller details, and the options and choices which inevitably lead to the right end result... a bit like when you are doing a jigsaw puzzle and you start off by finding the straight edges and corners first to give you a foundation to build it from.

This will show you how it all fits together.
Document <u>what</u> results are expected, <u>why</u> it is important and <u>how</u> it gets done.

Get the team member who is currently doing the job to record every step required to perform a task.

Once done, give the draft to other stakeholders the system impacts on for their examination and feedback on possible variables that may have been missed, and make the relevant adjustments.

Warning!! Don't get bogged down with exceptions.

Focus on systemising the routine.... And humanise the exceptions.

You can cover 80% of the eventualities with 20% of the effort, then with the remaining 20% - you'll find you are able to create further systems to cover those, but get the routine sorted first.

Also... Not too dumbed down.

Make it "Cake Box" simple. Write as though the reader does have the ability to do the job comfortably...once they have been shown once. Imagine how instructions on a Cake box are usually down to some basic steps, and they credit the reader with an average level of intelligence.

Reserve the detailed explanations for where they are crucial or the process will be too hard to follow when they need to refer back to it for a reminder.

Add the detail to the Procedure
When producing the procedure apply the KISS Principle – Keep It Simple, Stupid. Ensure you keep it as simple as it can be, but as detailed as it needs to be to get the job done properly.

Use visuals whenever possible and use language and terminology that everyone who needs to can understand and put into practice. Tie the detail here to the appropriate steps in the flow chart.

Consider these points in order to write successful procedures:
- Use numbered paragraphs to show that order is important

- Use bulleted paragraphs to list items that do not need to be completed in a specific order

What To Use?
By now I guess you are thinking – what do I use to create all this... it sounds like a lot of work. True... but just think back to the costs of inefficiency that we worked out earlier to give yourself the momentum you need – a job worth doing, is worth doing well... and trust me this is a job worth doing.

Think first, how are the intended users going to want to access it. Are they sitting in an office, or out in the field, or in the factory? Many won't want to be carrying around the good old-fashioned printed manual – who reads them anyway? Imagine you have a tradesperson out on site that needs to refer to a "how-to" efficiently. Would they like to just grab their mobile and do a quick search, or go back to their truck and see what they can find?

How much more useful is it going to be for them to watch a quick video explaining something that they have found in your privately shared "cloud" storage file.

There is simple and effective software that controls this for you easily keeping the version control up to date too as well as enabling users to find the right information easily – whether it is pdf, video, audio or some other format that suits you. I use a web knowledge base platform called TKO for all of this.

Don't always blame the people, blame the system first…. and look for where it can be tightened.

Kaizen, Kanban, 5S, Lean & Agile systems

When you start working in this space you'll potentially hear some jargon and different models. There are a number of methodologies around that help with developing your systems for efficiency, which I have been using for years without actually giving them a label.

In essence I have simplified the processes I have been using here for you to take and run with. It's not all that complicated when broken down into these simple steps and don't let the jargon confuse you. They are good and simple models that help your end game.

In very brief summary here's what they are about….

5S
This is about giving yourself a clean and tidy workspace. The 5 "S"s are –
1. Sort – what you need daily, and what you don't
2. Set – items in easily retrievable places depending on their frequency of use
3. Shine – be an expert at this consistently

4. Standardise – Use RACI (see Chapter 10) to ensure it is embraced by all
5. Sustain – Implement and keep the focus

Kaizen
Kaizen (usually pronounced 'kyzan' or 'kyzen' in the western world) is a Japanese word, commonly translated to mean 'continuous improvement' - a very significant concept within quality management

Kaizen is a way of thinking, working and behaving, embedded in the philosophy and values of the organization. Kaizen should be 'lived' rather than imposed or tolerated, at all levels.

The aims of a Kaizen organization are typically defined as:

- To be profitable, stable, sustainable and innovative.
- To eliminate waste of time, money, materials, resources and effort and increase productivity.
- To make incremental improvements to systems, processes and activities before problems arise rather than correcting them after the event.
- To create a harmonious and dynamic organization where every employee participates and is valued.

"**Every**" is a key word in Kaizen: improving everything that everyone does in every aspect of the organization in every department, every minute of every day. Evolution rather than revolution: continually making small, 1% improvements to 100 things is more effective, less disruptive and more sustainable than improving one thing by 100% when the need becomes unavoidable.

Understanding processes is essential before attempt is made to improve them. This is a central aspect to Total Quality Management, and also to more modern quality and process improvement interpretations and models such as Six Sigma

Kanban

Japanese for signboard or billboard, is a scheduling system for lean manufacturing and just-in-time (JIT) manufacturing and warehousing. Kanban is an inventory-control system to control the supply chain developed by Taiichi Ohno, an industrial engineer at Toyota, to improve manufacturing efficiency. It became an effective tool to support running a production system as a whole, and an excellent way to drive improvement. Problem areas are highlighted by reducing the number of kanban cards in circulation. One of the main benefits of kanban is to establish an upper limit to the work in process inventory, avoiding overloading of the manufacturing system.

Kanban cards are a key component of kanban and they signal the need to move materials within a production facility or to move materials from an outside supplier into the production facility. The kanban card is, in effect, a message that signals depletion of product, parts, or inventory. When received, the kanban triggers replenishment of that product. As such, consumption drives demand for more production, and the kanban card signals demand for more product—so kanban cards help create a demand-driven system.

One key indicator of the success of production scheduling based on demand, *pushing,* is the ability of the demand-forecast to create such a *push*. Kanban, is part of an approach where the "pull" comes from demand. Re-supply or production is determined according to the actual demand of the customer. In contexts where supply time is lengthy and demand is difficult to forecast, often, the best one can do is to respond quickly to observed demand. This situation is exactly what a kanban system accomplishes, in that it is used as a demand signal that immediately travels through the supply chain. This ensures that intermediate stocks held in the supply chain are better managed, and are usually smaller. Where the supply response is not quick enough to meet actual demand fluctuations, thereby causing potential lost sales, stock building may be deemed to be more effective, and is achieved by placing more kanban in the system. It is widely held by proponents of lean production and manufacturing that demand-driven systems lead to faster turnarounds in production and lower inventory levels, helping companies implementing such systems be more competitive. E-kanban is growing now as the electronic version as technology aids us.

Lean Six Sigma
A methodology that relies on a collaborative team effort to improve performance by systematically eliminating the eight kinds of waste: Transportation, Inventory, Motion, Waiting, Over Production, Over Processing, Defects, and Skills (abbreviated as 'TIMWOODS').

Lean Six Sigma utilizes the **DMAIC** (acronym for Define, Measure, Analyze, Improve and Control) phases similar to that of Six Sigma. Lean Six Sigma projects comprise aspects of Lean's waste elimination and the Six Sigma focus on reducing defects, based on Critical To **Quality (CTQ)** characteristics. The DMAIC toolkit of Lean Six Sigma comprises all the Lean and Six Sigma tools. Training for Lean Six Sigma is provided through the belt based training system similar to that of Six Sigma. The belt personnel are designated as white belts, yellow belts, green belts, black belts and master black belts. The skill sets reflect elements from Six Sigma, Lean and other process improvement methods like the **Theory Of Constraints (TOC)** and Total Productive Maintenance (TPM).

Agile project management is an "iterative" (repetitious) approach to planning and guiding project processes. An Agile project is completed in small sections called iterations. Each iteration is reviewed and critiqued by the project team, which may include representatives of the client business as well as employees. Insights gained from the critique of an iteration are used to determine what the next step should be in the project. Each iteration is normally scheduled to be completed within two weeks. The main benefit of Agile project management is its ability to respond to issues as they arise throughout the course of the project. Making a necessary change to a project at the right time can save resources and, ultimately, help deliver a successful project on time and within budget.

Because Agile management relies on the ability to make decisions quickly, it is not suitable for organizations that tend to deliberate over issues for a prolonged period or for those that take decisions to a committee.

Action Steps:
Have a practice here... draw up a simple flowchart of how you would make a cup of coffee...then ask someone else to follow it.

Chapter 8

Collaboration

Put the Team To Work

There are many ways and many benefits that collaboration will add to efficiencies and reduce waste. Here is where you need to decide who, where, what, when and how you can collaborate.

Why?

Collaboration is where you get real leverage towards achieving economies and efficiencies. In this digital age there are so many tools available to allow everyone to work together, yet remotely on projects, as well as an ongoing basis. The way of working is shifting and those who don't move with it – or even better – lead the change, will be left behind.

Businesses can share the load by working smarter together. Collaboration brings the advantages of accessing different skill sets, or machinery, or innovations to enhance their offerings, maybe as a joint venture, or simply by working together in strong alliances. An example of this is with the growth of cloud base software available to us now, there are specialist applications developed by separate companies designed to work in with other applications to enhance the complete package and allow the consumer to buy just what they need.

Xero Accounting is a case in mind where they don't try to provide everything a business will want in accounting or bookkeeping, but aim first to make the bookkeeping as efficient as possible, opening up and working collaboratively with add-on products that better handle stock-control, staff rostering or project management and sync cleanly between each other to save duplication of effort. There are many others such as MailChimp and a range of CRM packages that also work this way including tools at the larger end of town that plug in with SAP and similar tools to achieve an outcome of efficiency.

How?

There are of course many software tools that on their own are designed to encourage collaboration – or more importantly – efficiency in collaboration. When a team is working together and may or may not be in different locations, a tool that keeps everyone live and up to date and on the same page to avoid unnecessary meetings, or other reporting type communications can save many hours a week across an organisation.

You can research to find one that suits you. I use [Smartsheet](#) a lot which is essentially a task or project management tool which can be shared to any number of users in a team of collaborators. It is a spreadsheet style interface which is easily understood, and has the facility to emailing on a line by line basis to the accountable team member... things like reminders, notifications of updates or changes, requests for updates, sharing attachments, and discussion notes and more. Easily created Web forms allow other parties to enter data that you want to collect. It also has the ability to interface with other software.

Who can you collaborate with?

Collaboration involves close cooperation, clarity of shared goals, and a structured system of discussion and action to achieve them. Collaborative methods are useful for everything from group projects at school to community initiatives involving several organizations. Whether you're trying to form a collaboration between two groups or trying to get an individual member to pull his weight, there are many established ways to resolve conflict and achieve results.

The process is similar across the board and with the aim of collaboration being a win-win situation for everyone, you need to consider all possibilities for collaboration. This could be with key clients, valued suppliers, core team members and of course strategic alliances. Exploring with them opportunities to work together to a mutual advantage can bring huge benefits and stronger, longer lasting and more cost effective relationships. You might have a plan to improve your supply chain management, some product development, internal systems or smarter marketing options. Having key people close to you in core roles can save a mountain of time and investment when brainstorming new ideas, or to get feedback for specific issues that need addressing.

10 Tips for Quality Collaboration

1. **Understand the exact goal and timeline.** The purpose of collaboration should be obvious to all participants. Even when simply working on a short-term goal, make sure the exact scope of the project is known. Set specific and measureable targets that everyone understands and agrees with.
2. **Make Meetings Efficient.** Make good use of technology where possible. Use web-conference facilities and on-line project collaboration tools where possible. Keep a tight agenda to each meeting with notes and commitments made for future accountability.
3. **Help delegate tasks.** Rather than trying to do everything, it is best to divide and conquer. Let everyone find his or her strength and work to them. Clarity of roles is key as in any team. If you feel overwhelmed or think someone else could use your help, speak up.
4. **Let everyone participate in discussion.** Stop and listen if you find you talk more than most other participants. Collaboration thrives when each member recognizes the value of each other member's participation. Encourage quiet members to speak up, by asking them for input on a subject they are knowledgeable about.

5. **Trust Your Collaborators.** Have faith and trust their experience. Collaborative work proceeds most effectively in an atmosphere of trust. If you think someone is not acting in the group's best interest, you should try to discuss the reasons behind their actions without judgement. If you point a finger mistakenly, the spirit of collaboration can easily turn sour. Discuss problems openly, not behind a team-mate's back.
6. **Suggest ways to communicate.** Make sure there are opportunities for Collaborators to exchange ideas and information between meetings. Use online forums, email discussions, or document sharing services to keep members up to date. Meet as a group for the occasional relaxed gathering as well. You'll work better together when you know each other better.
7. **Hold team members accountable.** All team members should meet as a group to discuss ways to improve. Keep regular short-term milestones discussing how to meet them if you fall behind. Longer-term collaborations need regular check in for progress toward the eventual goal. Fact-based metrics are best for monitoring progress. For research accountabilities, you could review how many pages of notes they took or which sources they identified.
8. **Seek consensus whenever possible.** Disagreements are common in any group effort so seek consensus from all members on a decision. If you can't reach consensus and need to move forward, at least make sure disagreeing members accept that the group has made a reasonable effort to compromise or it will make further collaboration much harder.
9. **Don't burn any bridges.** Keep your emotions reigned in and forgive people who argue with you. Well-timed use of humor can be great for defusing a situation. Use self-deprecating humor or inoffensive jokes only, and don't offend someone by joking around when they're seriously upset.
10. **Reward Exceptional Outcomes.**
    While it is important to set clear goals, it is even more important to outline the rewards of good performance.

Rather than Management by Exception, reward higher performances. This could be as easy as taking them to lunch. Or even easier, just saying "well done" more often

Happy Collaborating!

Chapter 9

Innovation

A System for The Right Thinking

Success is a choice. I've always lived by the motto – "If It Is To Be, It Is Up To Me". No-one is going to do it for you, you need to make your own success, so wasting your time thinking of reasons for your failures and shortcomings is futile. Realise instead that the seeds of success were planted within you when you were born. YOU are responsible, not your mother, not your father, not society, not your competitors and certainly not the circle of friends or business associates you hang around... just YOU.

What has this to do with systemising your way to success you might ask? The seeds, and the power to grow them, are contained in the most awesome machine ever created: the human mind. No computer can come close to duplicating the goal setting, goal seeking, goal-attaining mechanism of the human mind. Success is a choice and not a chance. YOU were born a winner. YOU were born rich. YOU can be a success if only YOU make the right choice.

"Success is not reserved only for extraordinarily gifted people, it is available for those who seek it with a commitment and vision." So it goes without saying that we need to have a system to ensure that we maximize the potential of that powerful system in our heads.

Everything happens as a result of something. If we can identify the cause, we can control the effect. Thoughts and beliefs cause everything. We are responsible for what we choose to think and believe. We generally rise to the level that we expect. So we must set our expectations. Our success is dependent upon our level of confidence.

We are responsible for thinking confidently about ourselves and the attainment of our goals. Whatever the conscious mind accepts as true and chooses to believe, the subconscious will be driven to achieve. We are responsible for what we consciously choose to accept and believe. Our attitudes and actions are a result of habits ingrained in us over a period of time. We are responsible for either reinforcing good habits or unlearning bad habits and consciously replacing them with consistently practiced good habits.

We need to find, plant, and nurture the seeds that contain future success, in all areas of your life, whether they be financial, physical, emotional, or spiritual. **If YOU fail to accept this basic tenet, no success system or formula will pull you out of the hole you have dug for yourself.**

"If you think you can or if you think you can't, whichever way is right"

The 1%

Kaizen...a system of continuous improvement in quality, technology, processes, company culture, productivity, safety and leadership was created in Japan following World War II. The word Kaizen means "continuous improvement". It comes from the Japanese words "Kai" meaning school and "Zen" meaning wisdom.

Kaizen is a <u>system</u> that involves every employee - from upper management to the cleaning crew. Everyone is encouraged to come up with small improvement suggestions on a regular basis. This is not a once a month or once a year activity. It is continuous. In Japanese companies, such as Toyota and Canon, a total of 60 to 70 suggestions per employee per year are written down, shared and implemented.

In most cases these are not ideas for major changes. Kaizen is based on making little changes on a regular basis: always improving productivity, safety and effectiveness while reducing waste. 1% here, 1% there...it all adds up.

Suggestions are not limited to a specific area such as production or marketing. Kaizen is based on making changes anywhere that improvements can be made. Western philosophy may be summarized as, "if it ain't broke, don't fix it." The Kaizen philosophy is to "do it better, make it better, improve it even if it isn't broken, because if we don't, we can't compete with those who do."

Kaizen in Japan is a system of improvement that includes both home and business life. Kaizen even includes social activities. It is a concept that is applied in every aspect of a person's life.

In business, Kaizen encompasses many of the components of Japanese businesses that have been seen as a part of their success. Quality circles, automation, suggestion systems, just-in-time delivery, Kaizen involves setting standards and then continually improving those standards. To support the higher standards Kaizen also includes providing the training, materials and supervision that is needed for employees to achieve the higher standards and maintain their ability to meet those standards on an on-going basis.

By implementing a Kaizen style thinking system into your business you'll be sharing the load.... introducing leverage into your improvement process. It doesn't have to be just you that pulls it all together.

Six Thinking Hats

"Six Thinking Hats" introduced by Edward De Bono in the 50's is a powerful technique that helps you look at important decisions from a number of different perspectives. It helps you make better decisions by pushing you to move outside your habitual ways of thinking therefore helping you understand the full complexity of a decision, and spot issues and opportunities which you might otherwise not notice.

Many successful people think from a very rational, positive viewpoint, and this is part of the reason that they are successful. Often, though, they may fail to look at problems from emotional, intuitive, creative or negative viewpoints. This can mean that they underestimate resistance to change, don't make creative leaps, and fail to make essential contingency plans. Similarly, pessimists may be excessively defensive, and those used to a very logical approach to problem solving may fail to engage their creativity or listen to their intuition.

If you look at a problem using the Six Thinking Hats technique, then you'll use all of these approaches to develop your best solution. Your decisions and plans will mix ambition, skill in execution, sensitivity, creativity and good contingency planning.

To use Six Thinking Hats to improve the quality of your decision-making, look at the decision "wearing" each of the thinking hats in turn. Each "Thinking Hat" is a different style of thinking.

- **White Hat:** Focus on the data available. Look at the information you have, and see what you can learn from it. Look for gaps in your knowledge, and either try to fill them or take account of them.
- **Red Hat:** Look at the decision using intuition, gut reaction, and emotion, and try to understand the intuitive responses of people who do not fully know your reasoning.
- **Black Hat:** Look at things pessimistically, cautiously and defensively. Try to see why ideas and approaches might not work. This is important because it highlights the weak points in a plan or course of action.

- **Yellow Hat:** Think positively. It is the optimistic viewpoint that helps you to see all the benefits of the decision and the value in it, and spot the opportunities that arise from it.
- **Green Hat:** This is where you can develop creative solutions to a problem. It is a freewheeling way of thinking, in which there is little criticism of ideas.
- **Blue Hat:** Stands for process control. This is the hat worn by people chairing meetings. When running into difficulties because ideas are running dry, they may direct activity into Green Hat thinking. When contingency plans are needed, they will ask for Black Hat thinking.

You can use Six Thinking Hats in meetings or on your own. In meetings it has the benefit of defusing the disagreements that can happen when people with different thinking styles discuss the same problem.

For Example: The directors of a property company are looking at whether they should construct a new office building. The economy is doing well, and the amount of vacant office space is reducing sharply. As part of their decision they decide to use the 6 Thinking Hats technique during a planning meeting.

- **White Hat...** they analyse the data they have. They examine the trend in vacant office space, which shows a sharp reduction. They anticipate that by the time the office block would be completed, that there will be a severe shortage of office space. Current government projections show steady economic growth for at least the construction period.
- **Red Hat...** some of the directors think the proposed building looks quite ugly. While it would be highly cost-effective, they worry that people would not like to work in it.
- **Black Hat...** they worry that government projections may be wrong. The economy may be about to enter a 'cyclical downturn', in which case the office building may be empty for a long time. If the building is not attractive, then

companies will choose to work in another better-looking building at the same rent.
- **Yellow Hat...** if the economy holds up and their projections are correct, the company stands to make a great deal of money. If they are lucky, maybe they could sell the building before the next downturn, or rent to tenants on long-term leases that will last through any recession.
- **Green Hat...** they consider whether they should change the design to make the building more pleasant. Perhaps they could build prestige offices that people would want to rent in any economic climate. Alternatively, maybe they should invest the money in the short term to buy up property at a low cost when a recession comes.
- **Blue Hat...** has been used by the meeting's Chair to move between the different thinking styles. He or she may have needed to keep other members of the team from switching styles, or from criticizing other peoples' points.

Six Thinking Hats is a good technique for looking at the effects of a decision from a number of different points of view.

It allows necessary emotion and scepticism to be brought into what would otherwise be purely rational decisions. It opens up the opportunity for creativity within Decision Making. It also helps, for example, persistently pessimistic people to be positive and creative.

Plans developed using the '6 Thinking Hats' technique are sounder and more resilient than would otherwise be the case. This technique may also help you to avoid public relations mistakes, and spot good reasons not to follow a course of action, before you have committed to it.

Chapter 10

Smart Implementation

Making it all work

This is not a do it once and forget project. Your "Charter" is a living culture that needs to be alive throughout the organisation to be fully effective.

Pulling all the elements together is more of an organisation wide mentality and needs strong leadership to embed the benefits throughout.

The template here is designed to help convey the message simply and enable everyone to fully understand the aims of it within their own area of responsibility.

A Charter document should be established firstly for the whole organisation, and then departments or divisions and in many cases individuals can create their own that is in tune with the bigger picture.

Sometimes a division might want or need to be the pioneers simply to get a challenge addressed or to demonstrate the way for the rest of the business to follow.

Change Management Techniques…

Implementation can often involve requiring some change and this needs to be handled correctly. Much has been written about change management, but it's worth giving a quick mention here to the widely used "**RACI**" method.

RACI stands for Responsible, Accountable, Contribute, and Informed.

Responsible
The "doer" – whoever it is that has been made responsible for completion of the task.

Accountable
The person with their backside on the line. Often someone who the responsibility might ultimately lie with, but may not necessarily be doing the job.

Contribute
Can also be **"Consult"** and is the other parties involved who can help along the process of change, and may have valuable input to offer. This might be for example those up or down line of the process being systemised.

Informed
Is effectively just that, making sure that everyone is informed of the change. Recognising everyone affected and involved in any change is important to ensuring that any change is not undone by failing to involve or inform the relevant people.

Imagine thrusting a new system on to someone who wasn't involved with producing it, potentially they'll feel unworthy or disinterested... are they going to go out of their way to make it work?

This is probably a good time to look at potential roadblocks that you might need to be prepared for.

11 Potential Obstacles to Consider

Fore-warned is fore-armed. There are several potential pitfalls to implementing the Jonesci Charter for developing a lean and agile culture into a business. Many of these are inter-related so let's have a look at them now...

1. Resistance

Resistance can come from fear... not knowing why or how, and generally brought about by lack of or poor communication. Many just don't like change, and others may be happier knowing there is no focus... most likely at the expense of the business.

2. Nobody owning the process

As is often the case in any area of endeavour... if no-one is responsible, then it is left to chance whether or not something is achieved. If implementation and monitoring is made the responsibility of someone then there is ownership and accountability to follow through.

3. People feeling excluded

Don't just pick one person in the team to help without the inclusion of the others. Certainly you can have one person work on it initially, but it is important that the rest of the team are informed that the Charter plans will be discussed with them for their inclusion and feedback. For economical reasons, of course you don't want everyone on the team spending time on the whole process, so a good idea is to let others know this and understand they will be given the opportunity to contribute their thoughts at the relevant time.

4. High expectations from management with low support

Team members are usually willing to help develop the business especially where management takes the time to support that team member. Don't just leave them to it without giving them the resources or time required to complete it properly.

5. Loss of Momentum

Many a great opportunity is lost to us, through the daily demands of business. Often this is due to lack of one thing... prioritising in a weekly plan. Whilst in the initial phase people will generate their own momentum, after time passes other things take precedence and momentum is lost. However, with some goals, a plan, tracking, and recognition can be maintained. Another challenge is being too ambitious with the goals in the beginning and not achieving them, so this can slow momentum even more.

6. Management Sabotaging the Charter
If management takes short-cuts or bends the rules, it sends the message to everyone else that the Charter is not that important, so instantly diminishes the value of it... This could affect not only that particular part of the Charter, but other parts too may be affected by this mindset, so <u>everyone</u> needs to follow it.

7. Lack of Tracking or Celebration
Catch people doing the right thing. When was the last time you got up in the morning and set out to do something wrong at work?

Probably never if you are like 99% of the population... people try to do the right thing, *(some maybe don't try that hard)* and they like to hear they are doing the right thing. So often though, they only hear when they have done the wrong thing... so get negative feedback. Remember that positive reinforcement produces positive results.

8. Poor Communication
If something goes wrong, look first to the system for the problem and not the person. More often than not roles and systems to follow are either poorly introduced or simply "abdicated". By following a proper process to train and implement changes or new systems the likelihood of the team being able to do things correctly will increase.

9. Personality Styles
Probably a totally separate subject to cover, but it is important to recognise that as humans we all have different styles. Some just love the detail, whilst the more creative and impulsive among us like the freedom to do as they will. Our Charter needs to recognise this and be kept simple enough to follow without being restrictive.

10. Learning Styles

Remember to use the most appropriate medium to show the team, such as using audio, video, pictures, charts, and diagrams to cover everyone's different learning styles.

11. Charters not being kept up to date

Simply... if you make a change, then update the Charter and communicate it. Also, make sure that there is only one version of it in circulation, so everyone is working on the same page. Version tracking should be used as a safeguard so everyone knows they have the current issue.

So there you have it – the process behind creating your own JONESCI Charter.

It's pretty simple, but not necessarily "easy". Take your time to do it properly and don't take short cuts. Your business is still running, so it doesn't have to be done today...or tomorrow.

Small Steps – Big Results
Just think 12 months ahead and how your business could be performing with a Charter. What are the benefits you will be enjoying?

Now think what it could be like if you don't start now – possibly the same as it is now? How much time, energy and profits would you have wasted in that year?

Let me know how you go.
I'd love to hear from you... share with me the successes you've had from creating your Charter...remember... business should be plain sailing!

If you need help, let me know.

Clive Jones.
Turbocharging Business Systematically – so life can be plain sailing

How We Help With Productivity, Proficiency & Profitability

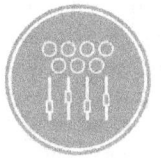

All Systems Go Coaching
1 to 1, Group and Mastermind

Yacht Based Retreats
Structured Small Group Development
Implementation Accountability

Efficiency Tools
Supply Relationship Management
Policies & Procedures
Projects and more...

Group Training
Workshops delivering Frameworks and Systems To Optimise Your Performance

The Leaky Bucket Challenge
Guaranteed to find you at least 20 X your investment.

We don't know what we don't know! We all know we should regularly go to a doctor for a thorough check-up, and we're better off finding out before it's too late if something needs attention…. But when was the last time you took time out to review how well your business was functioning? Are you haemorrhaging profits….internally and externally? Is time or money simply slipping through your fingers undetected?

This kind of thinking is often done at the time of a major milestone or when a critical decision has to be made... or simply in crisis mode… but why wait until then when you could benefit now?

Raise The Bar!
You are probably familiar with the term "Comfort Zones"… Just as the best in sport have their specialists to help them lift their game, business owners also need someone to help them lift theirs. Even the most successful businesses are haemorrhaging profits, some more than others, and through a wide range of potential inefficiencies, so our goal is to prevent that as much as we can.

As humans we get comfortable with what we are doing daily, and often miss those improvements by not stepping out and challenging occasionally, the comfort zones that we immerse ourselves in.

> "We have found about $100,000 through this review… It certainly was beneficial to have 'outside eyes' looking at my business and helping to point me in the right direction…" Graham

Tell-tale Signs Of Inefficiency
Businesses can experience or be at risk of diseconomies of scale in many ways. This can be through growth by acquisition of other businesses, booms in organic growth (new partner or investor or bank loan), adopting more products/services/market areas, or the securing of a major tender/supplier, loss of valuable management resources at the wrong time…and quite simply.. ineffective or poor systems and processes

to drive their business. Tell-tale signs that companies experience when these things occur include...
- Being late on delivery deadlines, and slow to react to client demands, or competitive threats.
- A rising cost of sale.
- Falling workforce morale including Management Stress through, Absenteeism, Decent or Fighting/conflict.
- Growth has stalled
- High levels of waste.
- Increasing debt

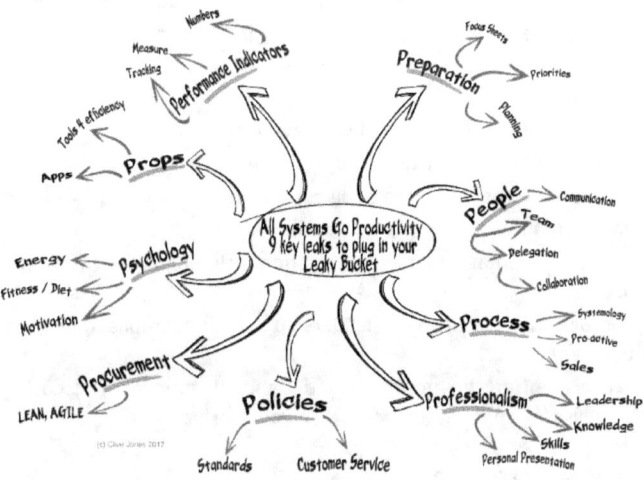

Is It For Me?
If you haven't analysed your business properly for a long time, if ever... now is _always_ a great time. However, **it's vital if you are experiencing any challenges already mentioned or are considering...**
- purchasing other companies.
- adding to the management team, or sales team... or taking on new partners,
- looking at investment loans or expansions to an overdraft,
- winning a large tender, or the distribution rights of a significant product or service
- consolidation from a Cash-flow management focus, or Work force and/or Supplier rationalisation.

- readying your business or business system for sale by franchising, or opening more branches
- or simply to maximise your returns in your exit strategy and succession planning

"It will help your business immensely"- **Scott**

How does it work?
We start with a series of questions and checklists to run through to review you and your business. Casting a systematic magnifying glass over the whole business to explore all avenues of opportunity for you to build upon, we will examine how well you have systemised...

- your goal setting and planning to take you to them,
- your financial management and your understanding of what it all means,
- the consistency of delivery of your goods or services,
- how you manage your time and yourself,
- everything to do with marketing your niche,
- and then how you convert this marketing into sales,
- your documentation and systemisation including the technology you use,
- and of course, your team, leadership and the complications that all that can involve.
- We also offer the option of independent supplier and customer surveys to gain their perspective on your business too.

You'll get some great ideas...
As part of this process you'll want to have a notepad handy as in the simple process of our asking some of these probing questions, you'll have some "Blinding Flashes of the Obvious" ... those little pots of gold that you'll want to rush away and implement straight away... but that's normal, let's just start by capturing them and then we'll help you pull them all together into your plan when the timing is right.

Is it complicated?
No, most of what we work on is not rocket science and you'll be able to answer most of the questions off the top of your head, though some may take a bit of research and highlight some areas that need to be worked on to bring into the business. Be prepared for some challenging questions too, but you'd expect that to grow you will need to take on some challenges.

What is the Outcome?
We compile an easy to understand report for you to keep and digest for implementing in your business. You'll also be given some options for your next steps to take to get some quick gains and solve some challenges. Our philosophy is to be there for you for the long haul... not just a quick fix... or even just a lot of promises.

Our Promise
We will identify a number of things that can be done to make you and your business more effective and efficient... but we don't leave you all excited and not knowing what to do next. The key thing is, that if we identify some decent opportunities for you... then our goal is to make sure you can capitalise on them, regardless of how much you want us to be involved.

20 x ROI Guarantee
If the process of the Leaky Bucket Challenge fails to identify the potential for at least 20 times the value of your investment, we will refund the entire investment in full, and still deliver your report at no further cost..!!

Take the Challenge Now – It's in your best interest.

About the Author:
Clive I. Jones (aka Jonesci)

35 years Business Management Experience including:
- 3 x Management troubleshooting jobs
- 4 year Business Apprenticeship
- Family of Small Business Owners...Father, Mother, Uncles, Father In Law,
- 4 years systemising Fathers Business
- 23 years in own businesses (incl. 4 different franchises)
- 7 years as software implementer/trainer
- 5 years Business Consultant
- 12+ years as Business & Executive Coach....
- 20+ years as a YachtMaster Instructor

Contact Clive and his team for any of the following:

Business Coaching & Consulting Programs
- 1 to 1 and Group Coaching
- Face to Face or by Phone or the most efficient Internet technologies
- Project based engagements to address a particular goal
- Turbocharged Business Tips & Book Reviews

The Ultimate Company Planning Retreats
- for small groups with a specific focus.
- More than simple Team Building this is a powerful Coaching environment for Managers and Owners wishing to make a real difference in the way they run their businesses.

Speaking Engagements and Workshops
- Guest speaker spots on tailored material to focus on your needs.
- Clive runs a very inclusive style of engagement drawing from the attendees as much as possible to encourage successful outcomes.
- In-house Workshops from ½ day to longer, with scheduled follow-up to ensure real benefit is gained through Implementation.
- All workshops leave the attendees with an action plan to take away and start working on.

Supply Chain Efficiency and Collaboration
- There are huge opportunities as you will have read in this book, in the whole Supply Chain.
- Clive has spent many years identifying and reducing wastage and over spending in this area of business.
- From Strategic Sourcing, to Compliance Management, Contract Management and Asset Management there are so many inefficiencies to be rectified.

www.ingramcontent.com/pod-product-compliance
Lightning Source LLC
Chambersburg PA
CBHW071216240526
45470CB00018B/1896